FAMINE,
AFFLUENCE,
AND
MORALITY

FAMINE,

AFFLUENCE,

AND

MORALITY

PETER SINGER

OXFORD
UNIVERSITY PRESS

OXFORD

UNIVERSITY PRESS

Oxford University Press is a department of the
University of Oxford. It furthers the University's objective
of excellence in research, scholarship, and education
by publishing worldwide.

Oxford   New York
Auckland   Cape Town   Dar es Salaam   Hong Kong   Karachi
Kuala Lumpur   Madrid   Melbourne   Mexico City   Nairobi
New Delhi   Shanghai   Taipei   Toronto

With offices in
Argentina   Austria   Brazil   Chile   Czech Republic   France   Greece
Guatemala   Hungary   Italy   Japan   Poland   Portugal   Singapore
South Korea   Switzerland   Thailand   Turkey   Ukraine   Vietnam

Oxford is a registered trade mark of Oxford University Press
in the UK and certain other countries.

Published in the United States of America by
Oxford University Press
198 Madison Avenue, New York, NY 10016

Library of Congress Cataloging-in-Publication Data
Singer, Peter, 1946- author.
Famine, affluence, and morality / Peter Singer.
pages   cm
Includes index.
ISBN 978-0-19-021920-8 (cloth : alk. paper)
1. Humanitarianism.   2. Famines—Moral and ethical aspects.
3. Poverty—Moral and ethical aspects.   4. Suffering—Moral and
ethical aspects.   5. Wealth—Moral and ethical aspects.   I. Title.
BJ1475.3.S56   2015
170—dc23   2015005676

9 8 7 6 5 4 3 2 1

Typeset in Miller Text Font
Printed in the United States of America
on acid-free paper

CONTENTS

FOREWORD

The world has improved dramatically in the more than forty years that have passed since Singer wrote "Famine, Affluence, and Morality." The proportion of the world's population living in extreme poverty today is less than half what it was then, and the proportion of children who die before their fifth birthday has plunged even more. In 1960, almost 20 percent of the world's children died before their fifth birthday. By 1990, it was around 10 percent, and now it's closer to 5 percent.

But 5 percent is still too many—on the order of 6.3 million child deaths a year. Most of these deaths are the result of conditions like diarrhea, pneumonia, or malaria that we know how to prevent or cure. Nevertheless, the reduction in child deaths is encouraging. It shows that aid does work and refutes the damaging myth that foreign aid does no good.

Singer's work argues that we can work together to prevent very bad things from happening—like the deaths of children. The evidence for this claim is much stronger now than it was in 1972. Fortunately, more and more people are seeing that this is the case, and many of them are also taking action. You might suggest that Singer's article was ahead of its time when it was originally published. But perhaps it's time has now come.

—Bill and Melinda Gates, co-chairs,
The Bill and Melinda Gates Foundation

PREFACE

"Famine, Affluence, and Morality" was written at the height of the refugee crisis brought about by military repression in what was then East Pakistan. Nine million people fled across the border into India, where they struggled to survive in refugee camps. With the benefit of hindsight, we can see the crisis as a pivotal stage in the emergence of Bangladesh as an independent nation, but at the time that fortunate outcome seemed improbable, whereas the immense number of people in peril was apparent. I used the dire emergency as a springboard for my argument that people in affluent nations should be doing much more to help people in great need in much poorer parts of the world, but that argument is quite general in its application, and the challenge it presents remains as confronting today as it was in 1971.

Ethics and political philosophy were then on the verge of an exciting new transformation. For the previous twenty-five years moral philosophy had focused on analyzing the meanings of moral terms like "good" and "ought" and this was assumed to have no implications for substantive questions about how we ought to live. A. J. Ayer wrote that it is a mistake to look to moral philosophers for guidance and Peter Laslett seemed to be summing up a widespread view with his oft-quoted line: "For the moment, anyway, political philosophy is dead."[1] That "moment" lasted until the student protest movement of the 1960s demanded courses that were relevant to the major issues of the day: civil rights, racial discrimination,

---

[1] A. J. Ayer, "The Analysis of Moral Judgment" in A. J. Ayer, *Philosophical Essays* (London: Macmillan, 1954). Around the time I was writing "Famine, Affluence, and Morality," I wrote a brief note critical of this view of the subject, published as "Moral Experts," *Analysis*, 32 (1972): 115–17. Peter Laslett's remark is from his introduction to his edited volume, *Philosophy, Politics and Society* (Oxford: Blackwell, 1956).

the war in Vietnam, and civil disobedience. Then some philosophers recalled that their tradition had, in previous eras, had a lot to say about these topics. The launch of a new journal *Philosophy & Public Affairs* was announced with a "Statement of Purpose" proclaiming that a philosophical examination of issues of public concern "can contribute to their clarification and their resolution." (Today, it is hard to believe that a statement so cautiously phrased could be regarded as radical.) Thus began, or rather was revived, the field now known as "practical" or "applied" ethics.

When the soon-to-be-launched journal began inviting the submission of papers, I was a recent Oxford graduate, just starting my first academic position. Already as an undergraduate in Australia I had been involved in the abortion law reform movement and the opposition to the war in Vietnam. At Oxford I had written my thesis on the basis of the obligation to obey the law in a democracy.[2] My wife and I were donating 10 percent of our income to Oxfam

---

[2] The thesis became the basis for my first book, *Democracy and Disobedience* (Oxford: Oxford University Press, 1973).

and had recently become vegetarian, after learning about how animals are treated before being turned into meat.[3] I was eager to tackle, in a philosophical way, the important ethical questions that I faced in my own life. The launch of *Philosophy & Public Affairs* provided the perfect opportunity to do so. "Famine, Affluence, and Morality" appeared in spring 1972, in the third issue of the first volume.

The article soon became a staple of courses in ethics. An incomplete list of anthologies in which it has been reprinted runs to fifty. Each year it is read by thousands of undergraduates and high school students in many different countries. Yet until recently, it was probably more often used to pose an intellectual puzzle rather than to challenge students to consider if they are living ethically. Professors presented it by saying: "Here is an article with an argument that seems to be sound, but the conclusion is impossibly demanding. Find the flaw in the argument." Over the past decade, however,

---

[3] I presented this argument in my second book, *Animal Liberation* (New York: New York Review/Random House, 1975).

more and more students, and at least some of their professors, took a different stance. They found no flaw in the argument and were keen to explore its ethical implications.[4] The emerging new movement known as Effective Altruism includes many people who have been influenced by the essay, or by the other writings in this book, to change their lives.[5] Here are a few examples:

• Toby Ord read the essay when he was a philosophy student. He went on to found Giving What We Can, which encourages people to pledge to give 10 percent of their pre-tax income, until retirement, to the charities that they believe will do the most good. Members of Giving What We Can have, at the time of writing, donated over £8 million and the pledges already made

---

[4] Joshua Greene described this shift in the approach taken to the article when introducing me prior to a talk I gave at Harvard University in April 2015 on behalf of Harvard Effective Altruism. Greene, who had been an undergraduate at Harvard, contrasted the approach his professor took to the article with that of the students who had organized the talk and those who had filled the large lecture theater to hear it.

[5] See Peter Singer, *The Most Good You Can Do* (New Haven: Yale University Press, 2015), and William MacAskill, *Doing Good Better* (New York: Gotham Books, 2015).

commit them to donating an estimated £457 million over their lifetimes.

• Chris Croy was assigned "Famine, Affluence, and Morality" for a class he took at St. Louis Community College, in Meramec, Missouri. The class also read an opposing essay in which the philosopher John Arthur argued that if my argument were sound, it would follow that we should also aid others by giving parts of our bodies, such as a kidney. Arthur held that this can't be right: the fact that more good will come from such a donation is not enough, he thought, to show that we ought to do it. To Croy, that seemed more like an argument for donating a kidney than against giving to people in extreme poverty. After thinking hard about it, and discussing it with a friend, he called a local hospital, and subsequently donated one of his kidneys to a stranger (who turned out to be a 43-year-old schoolteacher working at a school that serves mostly poor children).

• Gustav Alexandrie, a Swedish composer, was influenced by my writings to give to organizations helping the world's poorest people. He wanted to help spread the idea that he considered so important, and decided to use his own particular expertise to do so. He wrote a piece of choral music in which the choir sings about the central analogy of the article, the child drowning in the shallow pond. Alexandrie's composition was premiered in Stockholm in 2014 by the Södra Latin Chamber Choir, conducted by Jan Risberg.

• Dean Spears completed his PhD in economics in 2013. A few years earlier, he and his wife Diane Coffey, also studying for her doctorate at Princeton, had started an organization in India called Research Institute for Compassionate Economics or r.i.c.e (www.riceinstitute.org). After graduation, Dean made r.i.c.e.'s work his full-time job. As he put it in an email to me, his decision was "due to a process that largely started with 'Famine, Affluence, and Morality.'" The argument of that article was, however, importantly bolstered by Diane's longstanding commitment to a career of service to the poor. Dean and Diane now live in India and are focusing on the issue of open defecation, a problem that has been unduly neglected, perhaps because it seems embarrassing to discuss, but has a very severe impact on the health of young children, with consequences that can blight their adult lives as well. I'm pleased, of course, that my article could have led to Dean and Diane doing such important work. My favorite part of Dean's message, however, was a footnote saying: "We read from the pond story at our wedding."

• In January 2015, while I was writing this preface, I received an email from David Bernard, an undergraduate at Uppsala University, in Sweden, inviting me to speak at his university at a meeting to be arranged by the newly formed group Effective Altruism Uppsala. David then added a personal note: "'Famine, Affluence, and Morality' was the first step on my path to discovering effective altruism.... Your writings have helped me immensely in taking concrete actions to fulfil the vague desire I had to do good and have helped give my life much more meaning."

Now it's your turn to read "Famine, Affluence, and Morality." Perhaps it will change your life too. If you find it persuasive, please think about how you can help to spread its central idea.

◊

"Famine, Affluence, and Morality" has had its fair share of objections and counter-arguments—or perhaps rather more than its fair share, because it leads to the uncomfortable conclusion that very few of us are living fully ethical lives. One point on which a correction is needed relates to the estimated cost of saving a life by donating to a charity. The analogy between saving the child in the pond and saving the life of a child in a developing country dying from poverty-related causes implies that, for the cost of replacing one's muddy clothes one can save a life. In the second essay reprinted here, "The Singer Solution to World Poverty," I refer to Peter Unger's rough calculation that you can save a life for $200. In other places—among them, "What Should a Billionaire

Give—and What Should You?," which is also reprinted in this volume—I have imagined that wading into the pond to save the child will ruin your shoes, and that for the cost of an expensive pair of shoes, you could save a child's life.

One very welcome development in philanthropy since the publication of "Famine, Affluence, and Morality" is that today there is much more emphasis on evaluating what charities seeking to help the global poor actually achieve. A great deal of research has been done into the effectiveness of particular charities, enabling people to make better charitable choices and thus to do more good with the money that they donate. This research has shown that many early estimates of the cost of saving a life did not include all the costs involved, or were based on inaccurate estimates of how often a form of aid such as providing bednets to protect people against malaria actually saved a life.[6] GiveWell, which has led

---

[6] For a critique of the pond analogy on these grounds, see Jonah Sinick, "Some Reservations About Singer's Child-in-the-Pond Argument," at http://lesswrong.com/lw/hr5/some_reservations_about_singers_childinthepond/, accessed August 9, 2015.

the way in rigorously evaluating the cost-effectiveness of charities, estimates that although it costs the Against Malaria Foundation no more than $7.50 to provide and deliver a bednet to a family in a malaria-prone region of Africa, the cost of a life saved as a result of this distribution is $3,340. The difference reflects the fact that most bednets do not save lives (although some of them prevent debilitating but not fatal cases of malaria, as well as other diseases carried by mosquitoes). In general, GiveWell considers a cost of less than $5,000 per life saved an indication that a charity is highly cost-effective.[7] That figure is, for most of us, much more than the cost of our most expensive suit or shoes, so it was a mistake to compare that cost with what we would need to spend in order to save the life of a child at risk from poverty-related causes. It remains true, though, that most people who are middle class

---

[7] http://www.givewell.org/International/top-charities/amf. GiveWell considers anything under $5,000 per life saved to be good value, though the organization also cautions against taking such estimates too literally. For further discussion see http://www.givewell.org/international/technical/criteria/cost-effectiveness.

or above in affluent countries spend much more than $5,000 on items that are not of comparable moral significance to saving a life. Moreover as Unger has shown with his story of Bob and the Bugatti, which I retell in "The Singer Solution to World Poverty," our intuitive judgment in situations where we can save a child in front of us is that we should be prepared to sacrifice possessions worth much more than our clothes, and even more than $5,000. The change in the cost of saving a life does not, therefore, undermine the fundamental moral argument of "Famine, Affluence, and Morality."

I reply to some other objections in the two *New York Times* articles that are included in this volume, and further responses can be found in *Practical Ethics* and *The Life You Can Save*. Others have also defended the original argument; indeed there is now a considerable academic literature on the topic.[8] Rather than

---

[8] Peter Singer, *Practical Ethics*, 3rd ed. (Cambridge: Cambridge University Press, 2011); Peter Singer, *The Life You Can Save* (New York: Random House, 2009). For those wishing to pursue the current academic literature on the argument of "Famine Affluence, and Morality," a good place to start is Patricia Illingworth, Thomas Pogge, and Leif Wenar, eds., *Giving Well: The Ethics of Philanthropy*

go into this debate more deeply here, however, I want instead to broaden the discussion by mentioning some recent psychological research that helps us to understand why we respond as we do to the story of the child in the pond.

◊

Joshua Greene directs the Moral Cognition Lab in Harvard University's Department of Psychology, but before going into psychology he got a PhD in philosophy at Princeton University, so he knew all about the challenge posed by the example of the child in the pond. He was well aware of the difficulty of condemning a failure to aid the drowning child near to you while permitting a failure to aid the starving child far from you, and yet he knew that almost everyone intuitively judges the two cases very differently. He wanted to know why.

(Oxford: Oxford University Press, 2010), especially Elizabeth Ashford, "Obligations of Justice and Beneficence to Aid the Severely Poor," pp. 26–45, and Leif Wenar, "Poverty Is No Pond: Challenges for the Affluent," pp. 104–32. For a response to the essay by Wenar, see Theron Pummer, "Risky Giving," at http://blog.practicalethics.ox.ac.uk/2015/01/risky-giving/, accessed January 13, 2015.

As I originally presented the example, there are several potentially significant differences between the two situations. The child in the pond is near to you, and presumably a member of your own community, whereas the starving child is far away, and a foreigner. A child falling into a pond is a rare emergency, whereas global poverty is an ongoing problem. There is just one, identifiable child in the pond needing to be rescued, and you can save that child, whereas there are millions of impoverished children dying from poverty-related causes each year, and you can't save them all, or even identify a particular child who will die if you do not help. You are the only one who can save the child in the pond, but any moderately affluent person can help children in poverty, so the responsibility for saving those children is diffused in a way that the responsibility for saving the child in the pond is not. And in the pond case you can see for yourself that your action is very likely to save a life, whereas when you donate to an aid organization you have to rely on information gathered by someone else about the likely impact of your donation. Is the difference in our intuitive judgments based more heavily on some of these factors than others? If we can answer that question, the answer may tell us something about the reliability of our intuitive judgments.

Greene worked with Jay Musen, a student, to test people's responses to various imaginary scenarios. The factor that had the biggest effect by far turned out to be the physical distance between the child and the person who could help. In one of the scenarios, you are vacationing in a developing country when it is hit by a devastating typhoon. You are safe, tucked away in a well-stocked cottage in the hills, but on the coast that your cottage overlooks, people are in desperate need of food, sanitation, and medical supplies. Relief efforts are underway, and you can donate money to help them reach more people. In response to this story, 68 percent said that you have a moral obligation to donate. In a different version, everything is the same except that it isn't you who is in the developing country, but your friend. You are at home, on your computer, when your friend contacts you, describing the situation and using his smartphone to give you a live audiovisual tour of the devastated area and the relief efforts, so that you can share his experience of being there. Again, you can help by donating, which you can do instantly, online, with your credit card. Note that in these two scenarios what Greene refers to (with some justification) as "the mess in Singer's original hypothetical" has been cleaned up.[9] You have the same information and the same ability to help. Other differences that exist between jumping into a pond to save a particular, presumably local, child and donating to an international aid organization to save one of many foreign children in need have also been eliminated. Yet in the second scenario, only 34 percent said that you have a moral obligation to help. Physical distance, it seems, is what is making the difference.[10]

---

[9] "Deep Pragmatism: A Conversation with Joshua D. Greene," August 30, 2013, http://edge.org/conversation/deep-pragmatism.

[10] Jonas Nagel and Michael Waldmann, of the University of Göttingen, in Germany, also tested for the factors that lead to the variations in responses to the drowning child and the child in poverty in a developing country, and reached a different conclusion, finding that

Greene argues that when we think about it, although we might make more severely negative judgments about the character of someone who allows a child to drown right in front of her because she is worried about having to buy a new suit than we would about the character of someone who does not help a child far away, physical distance can't really make a moral difference to what is right or wrong. What is going on, he suggests, is that we have "inflexible automatic settings" that determine our moral intuitions for most situations. It's like the difference between using automatic and manual modes on a camera. For most situations, the point-and-shoot mode works well enough, so why bother with setting the focus, aperture, and shutter speed manually? Most people don't. In

the directness of the information, rather than the physical distance, was the primary factor. (See Nagel and Waldmann, "Deconfounding Distance Effects in Judgments of Moral Obligation," *Journal of Experimental Psychology: Learning, Memory and Cognition* 39 (2013): 237–52.) Greene's research controlled for that factor and still found that distance makes a very substantial difference. Nevertheless, as Greene points out (*Moral Tribes* (New York: Penguin, 2013), 378, 261n), the conclusions that he draws from his research, and which I outline in the next paragraph, would hold just as well if directness of information is a significant factor in our responses.

moral reasoning, we also have two possible ways of reaching decisions. We have evolved moral intuitions that give us quick but inflexible responses to common situations, and we have our general capacities for reasoning that enable us to work out solutions from scratch. Because we evolved in small, face-to-face societies in which a child in front of us needing help might well be kin, or the child of someone with whom we have an ongoing connection, we evolved an emotional response that leads us to think that to refuse to help a child right in front of you would be monstrous. For virtually all of our evolutionary history, however, there was no possibility of even being aware of children far from us who were in need of help, let alone of helping them. So we never developed an emotional response to failing to help distant strangers. To consider that issue, we have to go into manual mode and use our reasoning capacities to decide what we ought to do.[11]

---

[11] See Joshua Greene, *Moral Tribes*. The camera analogy is first presented on page 15 and more fully developed in Chapter 5.

On the basis of Greene's research, it is possible to see afresh what I was doing in "Famine, Affluence, and Morality." I began by appealing to our evolved "point-and-shoot" response to saving the drowning child, and then switched to "manual mode" to enable us to see that the differences between that case and the situation in which we find ourselves, with respect to distant children dying from avoidable, poverty-related causes do not justify the judgment that saving the drowning child is morally obligatory whereas helping the distant children is optional. As a philosophical argument, the article requires us to use our reasoning capacities, and from that perspective, we have to acknowledge that there is no justification for having such a strong intuitive condemnation in one situation, and no such response in the other one. From an evolutionary perspective, however, that's not surprising, because the characteristics that are selected for are those that conduce to our survival and reproductive fitness, and helping distant strangers does not do that. Our capacity to reason is itself evolved, of course, yet it enables us to think beyond the limitations of our own survival and reproduction and reflect critically on the moral intuitions that evolution has bequeathed us.[12] Thus the evolutionary explanation of our intuitive judgment that there is a sharp moral difference between the two situations does not justify that intuitive judgment: on the contrary, it debunks it and tells us to think again.

◊

In 1971, I was concerned with a particular humanitarian crisis that threatened nine million people. Today the aim is to reduce extreme poverty, and the more than six million premature deaths that flow from it each year. That might seem like an insoluble problem, and this perception is itself a major obstacle to making progress against extreme poverty. What is the good of rescuing a child in a pond if more and more children are constantly

---

[12] This argument is elaborated in Katarzyna de Lazari-Radek and Peter Singer, *The Point of View of the Universe* (Oxford: Oxford University Press, 2014), especially Chapter 7.

falling in? As Bill and Melinda Gates have pointed out in their foreword, however, that is not the reality of the situation. We are making heartening progress in reducing extreme poverty, and in combating diseases like measles, malaria, and diarrhea, which are major killers of children in developing countries. More children are going to school, and as a result, are having fewer children, and are better able to care for the children they have. Interest in overcoming extreme poverty has never been higher. Never before have so many of the brightest university graduates dedicated themselves to discovering how best to overcome it. We cannot be satisfied with what has been achieved so far, but we can be encouraged by that achievement and we can reasonably hope to do even better in the decades to come.

ACKNOWLEDGMENTS

My greatest debt is to Renata, my wife, with whom I first discussed whether we ought to be sharing some of our income with people in need. Without her unhesitating support for that idea we would not have begun donating to Oxfam, and if we had not been doing that, I could not have written "Famine, Affluence, and Morality." Even then, I might never have written up my thoughts on this issue had not Ronald Dworkin encouraged me to submit an article to a new journal that would apply philosophy to issues of general concern. All of those involved in the launch of *Philosophy & Public Affairs* can therefore take some of the credit for the essay from which this book takes its title.

For the proposal to reprint the essay in book form, I am grateful to Peter Ohlin of Oxford University Press, and to Emily Sacharin and Gwen Colvin for their part in the production process. I also thank Bill and Melinda Gates for writing the foreword.

Finally, I turn to the many people who have made Effective Altruism an important part of their lives. Whether or not you have read "Famine, Affluence, and Morality," you have given new relevance to its central argument. You have shown that it is possible to treat it, not as a mere philosophical puzzle, but as a guide to how we ought to live.

FAMINE, AFFLUENCE, AND MORALITY

A s I write this, in November 1971, people are dying in East Bengal from lack of food, shelter, and medical care. The suffering and death that are occurring there now are not inevitable, not unavoidable in any fatalistic sense of the term. Constant poverty, a cyclone, and a civil war have turned at least nine million people into destitute refugees; nevertheless, it is not beyond the capacity of the richer nations to give enough assistance to reduce any further suffering to very small proportions. The decisions and actions of human beings can prevent this kind

Originally published in Philosophy and Public Affairs 1, no. 3 (Spring 1972): 229–43.

of suffering. Unfortunately, human beings have not made the necessary decisions. At the individual level, people have, with very few exceptions, not responded to the situation in any significant way. Generally speaking, people have not given large sums to relief funds; they have not written to their parliamentary representatives demanding increased government assistance; they have not demonstrated in the streets, held symbolic fasts, or done anything else directed toward providing the refugees with the means to satisfy their essential needs. At the government level, no government has given the sort of massive aid that would enable the refugees to survive for more than a few days. Britain, for instance, has given rather more than most countries. It has, to date, given £14,750,000. For comparative purposes, Britain's share of the nonrecoverable development costs of the Anglo-French Concorde project is already in excess of £275,000,000, and on present estimates will reach £440,000,000. The implication is that the British government values a supersonic transport more than thirty times as highly as it values the lives of the nine million refugees. Australia is another country which, on a per capita basis, is well up in the "aid to Bengal" table. Australia's aid, however, amounts to less than one-twelfth of the cost of Sydney's new opera house. The total amount given, from all sources, now stands at about £65,000,000. The estimated cost of keeping the refugees alive for one year is £464,000,000. Most of the refugees have now been in the camps for more than six months. The World Bank has said that India needs a minimum of £300,000,000 in assistance from other countries before the end of the year. It seems obvious that assistance on this scale will not be forthcoming. India will be forced to choose between letting the refugees starve or diverting funds from her own development program, which will mean that more of her own people will starve in the future.[1]

---

[1] There was also a third possibility: that India would go to war to enable the refugees to return to their lands. Since I wrote this essay, India has taken this way out. The situation is no longer that described above, but this does not affect my argument, as the next paragraph indicates.

These are the essential facts about the present situation in Bengal. So far as it concerns us here, there is nothing unique about this situation except its magnitude. The Bengal emergency is just the latest and most acute of a series of major emergencies in various parts of the world, arising both from natural and from manmade causes. There are also many parts of the world in which people die from malnutrition and lack of food independent of any special emergency. I take Bengal as my example only because it is the present concern, and because the size of the problem has ensured that it has been given adequate publicity. Neither individuals nor governments can claim to be unaware of what is happening there.

What are the moral implications of a situation like this? In what follows, I shall argue that the way people in relatively affluent countries react to a situation like that in Bengal cannot be justified; indeed, the whole way we look at moral issues—our moral conceptual scheme—needs to be altered, and with it, the way of life that has come to be taken for granted in our society.

In arguing for this conclusion I will not, of course, claim to be morally neutral. I shall, however, try to argue for the moral position that I take, so that anyone who accepts certain assumptions, to be made explicit, will, I hope, accept my conclusion.

I begin with the assumption that suffering and death from lack of food, shelter, and medical care are bad. I think most people will agree about this, although one may reach the same view by different routes. I shall not argue for this view. People can hold all sorts of eccentric positions, and perhaps from some of them it would not follow that death by starvation is in itself bad. It is difficult, perhaps impossible, to refute such positions, and so for brevity I will henceforth take this assumption as accepted. Those who disagree need read no further.

My next point is this: if it is in our power to prevent something bad from happening, without thereby sacrificing anything of comparable moral importance, we ought, morally, to do it. By "without sacrificing anything of comparable moral importance" I mean without causing anything else comparably bad to happen, or doing something that is wrong in itself, or failing to promote some moral good, comparable in significance to the bad thing that we can prevent. This principle seems almost as uncontroversial as the last one. It requires us only to prevent what is bad, and to promote what is good, and it requires this of us only when we can do it without sacrificing anything that is, from the moral point of view, comparably important. I could even, as far as the application of my argument to the Bengal emergency is concerned, qualify the point so as to make it: if it is in our power to prevent something very bad from happening, without thereby sacrificing anything morally significant, we ought, morally, to do it. An application of this principle would be as follows: if I am walking past a shallow pond and see a child drowning in it, I ought to wade in and pull the child out. This will mean getting my clothes muddy, but this is insignificant, while the death of the child would presumably be a very bad thing.

The uncontroversial appearance of the principle just stated is deceptive. If it were acted upon, even in its qualified form, our lives, our society, and our world would be fundamentally changed. For the principle takes, first, no account of proximity or distance. It makes no moral difference whether the person I can help is a neighbor's child ten yards from me or a Bengali whose name I shall never know, ten thousand miles away. Second, the principle makes no distinction between cases in which I am the only person who could possibly do anything and cases in which I am just one among millions in the same position.

I do not think I need to say much in defense of the refusal to take proximity and distance into account. The fact that a person is physically near to us, so that we have personal contact with him, may make it more likely that we *shall* assist him, but this does not show that we *ought* to help him rather than another who happens to be farther away. If we accept any principle of impartiality, universalizability, equality, or whatever, we cannot discriminate against someone merely because he is far away from us (or we are far away from him). Admittedly, it is possible that we are in a better position to judge what needs to be done to help a person near to us than one far away, and perhaps also to provide the assistance we judge to be necessary. If this were the case, it would be a reason for helping those near to us first. This may once have been a justification for being more concerned with the poor in one's town than with famine victims in India. Unfortunately for those who like to keep their moral responsibilities limited, instant communication and swift transportation have changed the situation. From the moral point of view, the development of the world into a "global village" has made an important, though still unrecognized, difference to our moral situation. Expert observers and supervisors, sent out by famine relief organizations or permanently stationed in famine-prone areas, can direct our aid to a refugee in Bengal almost as effectively as we could get it to someone in our own block. There would seem, therefore, to be no possible justification for discriminating on geographical grounds.

There may be a greater need to defend the second implication of my principle—that the fact that there are millions of other people in the same position, in respect to the Bengali refugees, as I am, does not make the situation significantly different from a situation in which I am the only person who can prevent something very bad from occurring. Again, of course, I admit that there is a psychological difference between the cases; one feels less guilty about doing nothing if one can point to others, similarly placed, who have also done nothing. Yet this can make no real difference to our moral obligations.[2] Should I consider that I am less

---

[2] In view of the special sense philosophers often give to the term, I should say that I use "obligation" simply as the abstract noun derived from "ought," so that "I have an obligation to" means no more, and no less, than "I ought to." This usage is in accordance with the definition of "ought" given by the Shorter Oxford English Dictionary: "the general verb to express duty or obligation." I do not think any issue of substance hangs on the way the term is used; sentences in

obliged to pull the drowning child out of the pond if on looking around I see other people, no farther away than I am, who have also noticed the child but are doing nothing? One has only to ask this question to see the absurdity of the view that numbers lessen obligation. It is a view that is an ideal excuse for inactivity; unfortunately most of the major evils—poverty, overpopulation, pollution—are problems in which everyone is almost equally involved.

The view that numbers do make a difference can be made plausible if stated in this way: if everyone in circumstances like mine gave £5 to the Bengal Relief Fund, there would be enough to provide food, shelter, and medical care for the refugees; there is no reason why I should give more than anyone else in the same circumstances as I am; therefore I have no obligation to give more than £5. Each premise in this argument is true, and the argu-

---

which I use "obligation" could all be rewritten, although somewhat clumsily, as sentences in which a clause containing "ought" replaces the term "obligation."

ment looks sound. It may convince us, unless we notice that it is based on a hypothetical premise, although the conclusion is not stated hypothetically. The argument would be sound if the conclusion were: if everyone in circumstances like mine were to give £5, I would have no obligation to give more than £5. If the conclusion were so stated, however, it would be obvious that the argument has no bearing on a situation in which it is not the case that everyone else gives £5. This, of course, is the actual situation. It is more or less certain that not everyone in circumstances like mine will give £5. So there will not be enough to provide the needed food, shelter, and medical care. Therefore by giving more than £5 I will prevent more suffering than I would if I gave just £5.

It might be thought that this argument has an absurd consequence. Since the situation appears to be that very few people are likely to give substantial amounts, it follows that I and everyone else in similar circumstances ought to give as much as possible, that is, at least up to the point at which by giving more one would begin to cause serious suffering for oneself and one's dependents—perhaps even beyond this point to the point of marginal utility, at which by giving more one would cause oneself and one's dependents as much suffering as one would prevent in Bengal. If everyone does this, however, there will be more than can be used for the benefit of the refugees, and some of the sacrifice will have been unnecessary. Thus, if everyone does what he ought to do, the result will not be as good as it would be if everyone did a little less than he ought to do, or if only some do all that they ought to do.

The paradox here arises only if we assume that the actions in question—sending money to the relief funds—are performed more or less simultaneously, and are also unexpected. For if it is to be expected that everyone is going to contribute something, then clearly each is not obliged to give as much as he would have been obliged to had others not been giving too. And if everyone is not acting more or less simultaneously, then those giving later will know how much more is needed, and will have no obligation to give more than is necessary to reach this amount. To say this is not to deny the principle that people in the same circumstances have the same obligations, but to point out that the fact that others have given, or may be expected to give, is a relevant circumstance: those giving after it has become known that many others are giving and those giving before are not in the same circumstances. So the seemingly absurd consequence of the principle I have put forward can occur only if people are in error about the actual circumstances—that is, if they think they are giving when others are not, but in fact they are giving when others are. The result of everyone doing what he really ought to do cannot be worse than the result of everyone doing less than he ought to do, although the result of everyone doing what he reasonably believes he ought to do could be.

If my argument so far has been sound, neither our distance from a preventable evil nor the number of other people who, in respect to that evil, are in the same situation as we are, lessens our obligation to mitigate or prevent that evil. I shall therefore take as established the principle I asserted earlier. As I have already said, I need to assert it only in its qualified form: if it is in our power to prevent something very bad from happening, without thereby sacrificing anything else morally significant, we ought, morally, to do it.

The outcome of this argument is that our traditional moral categories are upset. The traditional distinction between duty and charity cannot be drawn, or at least, not in the place we normally draw it. Giving money to the Bengal Relief Fund is regarded as an act of charity in our society. The bodies which collect money are known as "charities." These organizations see themselves in this way—if you send them a check, you will be thanked for your "generosity." Because giving money is regarded as an act of charity, it is not thought that there is anything wrong with not giving. The charitable man may be praised, but the man who is not charitable is not condemned. People do not feel in any way ashamed or guilty about spending money on new clothes or a new car instead of giving it to famine relief. (Indeed, the alternative does not occur to them.) This way of looking at the matter cannot be justified. When we buy new clothes not to keep ourselves warm but to look "well dressed" we are not providing for any important need. We would not be sacrificing anything significant if we were to continue to wear our old clothes and give the money to famine relief. By doing so, we would be preventing another person from starving. It follows from what I have said earlier that we ought to give money away, rather than spend it on clothes which we do not need to keep us warm. To do so is not charitable, or generous. Nor is it the kind of act which philosophers and theologians have called "supererogatory"—an act which it would be good to do, but not wrong not to do. On the contrary, we ought to give the money away, and it is wrong not to do so.

I am not maintaining that there are no acts which are charitable, or that there are no acts which it would be good to do but not wrong not to do. It may be possible to redraw the distinction between duty and charity in some other place. All I am arguing here is that the present way of drawing the distinction, which makes it an act of charity for a man living at the level of affluence which most people in the "developed nations" enjoy to give money to save someone else from starvation, cannot be supported. It is beyond the scope of my argument to consider whether the distinction should be redrawn or abolished altogether. There would be many other possible ways of drawing the distinction—for instance, one might decide that it is good to make other people as happy as possible, but not wrong not to do so.

Despite the limited nature of the revision in our moral conceptual scheme which I am proposing, the revision would, given the extent of both affluence and famine in the world today, have radical implications. These implications may lead to further objections, distinct from those I have already considered. I shall discuss two of these.

One objection to the position I have taken might be simply that it is too drastic a revision of our moral scheme. People do not ordinarily judge in the way I have suggested they should. Most people reserve their moral condemnation for those who violate some moral norm, such as the norm against taking another person's property. They do not condemn those who indulge in luxury instead of giving to famine relief. But given that I did not set out to present a morally neutral description of the way people make moral judgments, the way people do in fact judge has nothing to do with the validity of my conclusion. My conclusion follows from the principle which I advanced earlier, and unless that principle is rejected, or the arguments are shown to be unsound, I think the conclusion must stand, however strange it appears.

It might, nevertheless, be interesting to consider why our society, and most other societies, do judge differently from the way I have suggested they should. In a well-known article, J. O. Urmson suggests that the imperatives of duty, which tell us what we must do, as distinct from what it would be good to do but not wrong not to do, function so as to prohibit behavior that is intolerable if men are to live together in society.[3] This may explain the origin and continued existence of the present division between acts of duty and acts of charity. Moral attitudes are shaped by the needs of society, and no doubt society needs people who will observe the rules that make social existence tolerable. From the point of view of a particular society, it is essential to prevent violations of norms against killing, stealing, and so on. It is quite inessential, however, to help people outside one's own society.

If this is an explanation of our common distinction between duty and supererogation, however, it is not a justification of it. The moral point of view requires us to look beyond the interests of our own society. Previously, as I have already mentioned, this may hardly have been feasible, but it is quite feasible now.

---

[3] J. O. Urmson, "Saints and Heroes," in *Essays in Moral Philosophy*, ed. Abraham I. Melden (Seattle: University of Washington Press, 1958), 214. For a related but significantly different view see also Henry Sidgwick, *The Methods of Ethics*, 7th ed. (London: Dover Press, 1907), 220–21, 492–93.

From the moral point of view, the prevention of the starvation of millions of people outside our society must be considered at least as pressing as the upholding of property norms within our society.

It has been argued by some writers, among them Sidgwick and Urmson, that we need to have a basic moral code which is not too far beyond the capacities of the ordinary man, for otherwise there will be a general breakdown of compliance with the moral code. Crudely stated, this argument suggests that if we tell people that they ought to refrain from murder and give everything they do not really need to famine relief, they will do neither, whereas if we tell them that they ought to refrain from murder and that it is good to give to famine relief but not wrong not to do so, they will at least refrain from murder. The issue here is: Where should we draw the line between conduct that is required and conduct that is good although not required, so as to get the best possible result? This would seem to be an empirical question, although a very difficult one.

One objection to the Sidgwick-Urmson line of argument is that it takes insufficient account of the effect that moral standards can have on the decisions we make. Given a society in which a wealthy man who gives 5 percent of his income to famine relief is regarded as most generous, it is not surprising that a proposal that we all ought to give away half our incomes will be thought to be absurdly unrealistic. In a society which held that no man should have more than enough while others have less than they need, such a proposal might seem narrow-minded. What it is possible for a man to do and what he is likely to do are both, I think, very greatly influenced by what people around him are doing and expecting him to do. In any case, the possibility that by spreading the idea that we ought to be doing very much more than we are to relieve famine we shall bring about a general breakdown of moral behavior seems remote. If the stakes are an end to widespread starvation, it is worth the risk. Finally, it should be emphasized that these considerations are relevant only to the issue of what we should require from others, and not to what we ourselves ought to do.

The second objection to my attack on the present distinction between duty and charity is one which has from time to time been made against utilitarianism. It follows from some forms of utilitarian theory that we all ought, morally, to be working full time to increase the balance of happiness over misery. The position I have taken here would not lead to this conclusion in all circumstances, for if there were no bad occurrences that we could prevent without sacrificing something of comparable moral importance, my argument would have no application. Given the present conditions in many parts of the world, however, it does follow from my argument that we ought, morally, to be working full time to relieve great suffering of the sort that occurs as a result of famine or other disasters. Of course, mitigating circumstances can be adduced—for instance, that if we wear ourselves out through overwork, we shall be less effective than we would otherwise have been. Nevertheless, when all considerations of this sort have been taken into account, the conclusion remains: we ought to be preventing as much suffering as we can without sacrificing something else of comparable moral importance. This conclusion is one which we may be reluctant to face. I cannot see, though, why it should be regarded as a criticism of the position for which I have argued, rather than a criticism of our ordinary standards of behavior. Since most people are self-interested to some degree, very few of us are likely to do everything that we ought to do. It would, however, hardly be honest to take this as evidence that it is not the case that we ought to do it.

It may still be thought that my conclusions are so wildly out of line with what everyone else thinks and has always thought that there must be something wrong with the argument somewhere. In order to show that my conclusions, while certainly contrary to contemporary Western moral standards, would not have seemed so extraordinary at other times and in other places, I would like to quote a passage from a writer not normally thought of as a way-out radical, Thomas Aquinas.

> Now, according to the natural order instituted by divine providence, material goods are provided for the satisfaction of human needs. Therefore the division and appropriation of property, which proceeds from human law, must not hinder the satisfaction of man's necessity from such goods. Equally, whatever a man has in superabundance is owed, of natural right, to the poor for their sustenance. So Ambrosius says, and it is also to be found in the *Decretum Gratiani*: "The bread which you withhold belongs to the hungry; the clothing you shut away, to the naked; and the money you bury in the earth is the redemption and freedom of the penniless."[4]

I now want to consider a number of points, more practical than philosophical, which are

---

[4] *Summa Theologica*, II-II, Question 66, Article 7, in *Aquinas, Selected Political Writings*, ed. A. P. d'Entrèves, trans. J. G. Dawson (Oxford: Basil Blackwell, 1948), 171.

relevant to the application of the moral conclusion we have reached. These points challenge not the idea that we ought to be doing all we can to prevent starvation, but the idea that giving away a great deal of money is the best means to this end.

It is sometimes said that overseas aid should be a government responsibility, and that therefore one ought not to give to privately run charities. Giving privately, it is said, allows the government and the noncontributing members of society to escape their responsibilities.

This argument seems to assume that the more people there are who give to privately organized famine relief funds, the less likely it is that the government will take over full responsibility for such aid. This assumption is unsupported, and does not strike me as at all plausible. The opposite view—that if no one gives voluntarily, a government will assume that its citizens are uninterested in famine relief and would not wish to be forced into giving aid—seems more plausible. In any case, unless there were a definite probability that by refusing to give one would be helping to bring about massive government assistance, people who do refuse to make voluntary contributions are refusing to prevent a certain amount of suffering without being able to point to any tangible beneficial consequence of their refusal. So the onus of showing how their refusal will bring about government action is on those who refuse to give.

I do not, of course, want to dispute the contention that governments of affluent nations should be giving many times the amount of genuine, no-strings-attached aid that they are giving now. I agree, too, that giving privately is not enough, and that we ought to be campaigning actively for entirely new standards for both public and private contributions to famine relief. Indeed, I would sympathize with someone who thought that campaigning was more important than giving oneself, although I doubt whether preaching what one does not practice would be very effective. Unfortunately, for many people the idea that "it's the government's responsibility" is a reason for not giving which does not appear to entail any political action either.

Another, more serious reason for not giving to famine relief funds is that until there is effective population control, relieving famine merely postpones starvation. If we save the Bengal refugees now, others, perhaps the children of these refugees, will face starvation in a few years' time. In support of this, one may cite the now well-known facts about the population explosion and the relatively limited scope for expanded production.

This point, like the previous one, is an argument against relieving suffering that is happening now, because of a belief about what might happen in the future; it is unlike the previous point in that very good evidence can be adduced in support of this belief about the future. I will not go into the evidence here. I accept that the earth cannot support indefinitely a population rising at the present rate. This certainly poses a problem for anyone who thinks it important to prevent famine. Again, however, one could accept the argument without drawing the conclusion that it absolves one from any obligation to do anything to prevent famine. The conclusion that should be drawn is that the best means of preventing famine, in the long run, is population control. It would then follow from the position reached earlier that one ought to be doing all one can to promote population control (unless one held that all forms of population control were wrong in themselves, or would have significantly bad consequences). Since there are organizations working specifically for population control, one would then support them rather than more orthodox methods of preventing famine.

A third point raised by the conclusion reached earlier relates to the question of just how much we all ought to be giving away. One possibility, which has already been mentioned, is that we ought to give until we reach the level of marginal utility—that is, the level at which, by giving more, I would cause as much suffering to myself or my dependents as I would relieve by my gift. This would mean, of course, that one would reduce oneself to very near the material circumstances of a Bengali refugee. It will be recalled that earlier I put forward both a strong and a moderate version of the principle of preventing bad occurrences. The strong version, which required us to prevent bad things from happening unless in doing so we would be sacrificing something of comparable moral significance, does seem to require reducing ourselves to the level of marginal utility. I should also say that the strong version seems to me to be the correct one. I proposed the more moderate version—that we should prevent bad occurrences unless, to do so, we had to sacrifice something morally significant—only in order to show that, even on this surely undeniable principle, a great change in our way of life is required. On the more moderate principle, it may not follow that we ought to reduce ourselves to the level of marginal utility, for one might hold that to reduce oneself and one's family to this level is to cause something significantly bad to happen. Whether this is so I shall not discuss, since, as I have said, I can see no good reason for holding the moderate version of the principle rather than the strong version. Even if we accepted the principle only in its moderate form, however, it should be clear that we would have to give away enough to ensure that the consumer society, dependent as it is on people spending on trivia rather than giving to famine relief, would slow down and perhaps disappear entirely. There are several reasons why this would be desirable in itself. The value and necessity of economic growth are now being questioned not only by conservationists, but by economists as well.[5] There is no doubt, too, that the consumer society has had a distorting effect on the goals and purposes of its members. Yet looking at the matter purely from the point of view of overseas aid, there must be a limit to the extent to which we should deliberately slow down our economy; for it might be the case that if we gave away, say, 40 percent of our Gross National Product, we would slow

---

[5] See, for instance, John Kenneth Galbraith, *The New Industrial State* (Boston: Houghton Mifflin, 1967); and E. J. Mishan, *The Costs of Economic Growth* (New York: Praeger, 1967).

down the economy so much that in absolute terms we would be giving less than if we gave 25 percent of the much larger GNP that we would have if we limited our contribution to this smaller percentage.

I mention this only as an indication of the sort of factor that one would have to take into account in working out an ideal. Since Western societies generally consider 1 percent of the GNP an acceptable level for overseas aid, the matter is entirely academic. Nor does it affect the question of how much an individual should give in a society in which very few are giving substantial amounts.

◊

It is sometimes said, though less often now than it used to be, that philosophers have no special role to play in public affairs, since most public issues depend primarily on an assessment of facts. On questions of fact, it is said, philosophers as such have no special expertise, and so it has been possible to engage in philosophy without committing oneself to any position on major public issues. No doubt there are some issues of social policy and foreign policy about which it can truly be said that a really expert assessment of the facts is required before taking sides or acting, but the issue of famine is surely not one of these. The facts about the existence of suffering are beyond dispute. Nor, I think, is it disputed that we can do something about it, either through orthodox methods of famine relief or through population control or both. This is therefore an issue on which philosophers are competent to take a position. The issue is one which faces everyone who has more money than he needs to support himself and his dependents, or who is in a position to take some sort of political action. These categories must include practically every teacher and student of philosophy in the universities of the Western world. If philosophy is to deal with matters that are relevant to both teachers and students, this is an issue that philosophers should discuss.

Discussion, though, is not enough. What is the point of relating philosophy to public (and personal) affairs if we do not take our conclusions seriously? In this instance, taking our conclusion seriously means acting upon it. The philosopher will not find it any easier than anyone else to alter his attitudes and way of life to the extent that, if I am right, is involved in doing everything that we ought to be doing. At the very least, though, one can make a start. The philosopher who does so will have to sacrifice some of the benefits of the consumer society, but he can find compensation in the satisfaction of a way of life in which theory and practice, if not yet in harmony, are at least coming together.

THE SINGER SOLUTION TO WORLD POVERTY

"Not since 1940, when City College tried to hire an atheist and advocate of free love, Bertrand Russell, has an academic appointment created such a commotion."

That's how the *New York Times* reported on my move from Australia to the United States in 1999.[1] A coalition of anti-abortion and militant disability organizations, supported by Princeton University trustee Steve Forbes (at the time a candidate for

---

[1] Sylvia Nasar, "Princeton's New Philosopher Draws a Stir," *New York Times,* April 10, 1999.

Originally published in The New York Times Sunday Magazine, December 17, 2006.

the Republican nomination for president) demanded that my appointment be rescinded. The university stood firm on the principle of academic freedom, and all the protests achieved was to increase the interest in my writings. When the *New York Times Sunday Magazine* asked me to write for them, I used the opportunity to present an updated version of "Famine, Affluence, and Morality" to a vastly larger audience. The article included free phone numbers readers could call to donate to UNICEF or Oxfam America. UNICEF and Oxfam later told me that they had received, in the month following the article, a total of about $600,000 more than they usually took in over those phone lines. Years later, an Oxfam staff member told me, a woman came into her office, took a crumpled copy of the article out of her handbag, and said she wanted to donate. She subsequently became a major donor.

◊

n the Brazilian film "Central Station," Dora is a retired schoolteacher who makes ends meet by sitting at the station writing letters for illiterate people. Suddenly she has an opportunity to pocket $1,000. All she has to do is persuade a homeless 9-year-old boy to follow her to an address she has been given. (She is told he will be adopted by wealthy foreigners.) She delivers the boy, gets the money, spends some of it on a television set, and settles down to enjoy her new acquisition. Her neighbor spoils the fun, however, by telling her that the boy was too old to be adopted—he will be killed and his organs sold for transplantation. Perhaps Dora knew this all along, but after her neighbor's plain speaking, she spends a troubled night. In the morning Dora resolves to take the boy back.

Suppose Dora had told her neighbor that it is a tough world, other people have nice new TVs too, and if selling the kid is the only way she can get one, well, he was only a street kid. She would then have become, in the eyes of the audience, a monster. She redeems herself only by being prepared to bear considerable risks to save the boy.

At the end of the movie, in cinemas in the affluent nations of the world, people who would have been quick to condemn Dora if she had not rescued the boy go home to places far more comfortable than her apartment. In fact, the average family in the United States spends almost one-third of its income on things that are no more necessary to them than Dora's new TV was to her. Going out to nice restaurants, buying new clothes because the old ones are no longer stylish, vacationing at beach resorts—so much of our income is spent on things not essential to the preservation of our lives and health. Donated to one of a number of charitable agencies, that money could mean the difference between life and death for children in need.

◊

All of which raises a question: In the end, what is the ethical distinction between a Brazilian who sells a homeless child to organ peddlers and an American who already has a TV and upgrades to a better one—knowing that the money could be donated to an organization that would use it to save the lives of kids in need?

Of course, there are several differences between the two situations that could support different moral judgments about them. For one thing, to be able to consign a child to death when he is standing right in front of you takes a chilling kind of heartlessness; it is much easier to ignore an appeal for money to help children you will never meet. Yet for a utilitarian philosopher like myself—that is, one who judges whether acts are right or wrong by their consequences—if the upshot of the American's failure to donate the money is that one more kid dies on the streets of a Brazilian city, then it is, in some sense, just as bad as selling the kid to the organ peddlers. But one doesn't need to embrace my utilitarian ethic to see that, at the very least, there is a troubling incongruity in being so quick to condemn Dora for taking the child to the organ peddlers while, at the same time, not regarding the American consumer's behavior as raising a serious moral issue.

In his 1996 book, *Living High and Letting Die*, the New York University philosopher Peter Unger presented an ingenious series of imaginary examples designed to probe our intuitions about whether it is wrong to live well without giving substantial amounts of money to help people who are hungry, malnourished, or dying from easily treatable illnesses like diarrhea. Here's my paraphrase of one of these examples:

Bob is close to retirement. He has invested most of his savings in a very rare and valuable old car, a Bugatti, which he has not been able to insure. The Bugatti is his pride and joy. In addition to the pleasure he gets from driving and caring for his car, Bob knows that its rising market value means that he will always be able to sell it and live comfortably after retirement. One day when Bob is out for a drive, he parks the Bugatti near the end of a railway siding and goes for a walk up the track. As he does so, he sees that a runaway train, with no one aboard, is running down the railway track. Looking farther down the track, he sees the small figure of a child very likely to be killed by the runaway train. He can't stop the train and the child is too far away to warn of the danger, but he can throw a switch that will divert the train down the siding where his Bugatti is parked. Then nobody will be killed—but the train will destroy his Bugatti. Thinking of his joy in owning the car and the financial security it represents, Bob decides not to throw the switch. The child is killed. For many years to come, Bob enjoys owning his Bugatti and the financial security it represents.

Bob's conduct, most of us will immediately respond, was gravely wrong. Unger agrees. But then he reminds us that we, too, have opportunities to save the lives of children. We can give to organizations like UNICEF or Oxfam America. How much would we have to give one of these organizations to have a high probability of saving the life of a child threatened by easily preventable diseases? (I do not believe that children are more worth saving than adults, but since no one can argue that children have brought their poverty on themselves, focusing on them simplifies the issues.) Unger called up some experts and used the information they provided to offer some plausible estimates that include the cost of raising money, administrative expenses, and the cost of delivering aid where it is most needed. By his calculation, $200 in donations would help a sickly 2-year-old transform into a healthy 6-year-old—offering safe passage through childhood's most dangerous years. To show how practical philosophical argument can be, Unger even tells his readers that they can easily donate funds by using their credit card and calling one of these toll-free numbers: (800) 367-5437 for UNICEF; (800) 693-2687 for Oxfam America.

Now you, too, have the information you need to save a child's life. How should you judge yourself if you don't do it? Think again about Bob and his Bugatti. Unlike Dora, Bob did not have to look into the eyes of the child he was sacrificing for his own material comfort. The child was a complete stranger to him and too far away to relate to in an intimate, personal way. Unlike Dora, too, he did not mislead the child or initiate the chain of events imperiling him. In all these respects, Bob's situation resembles that of people able but unwilling to donate to overseas aid and differs from Dora's situation.

If you still think that it was very wrong of Bob not to throw the switch that would have diverted the train and saved the child's life, then it is hard to see how you could deny that it is also very wrong not to send money to one of the organizations listed above. Unless, that is, there is some morally important difference between the two situations that I have overlooked.

Is it the practical uncertainties about whether aid will really reach the people who need it? Nobody who knows the world of overseas aid can doubt that such uncertainties exist. But Unger's figure of $200 to save a child's life was reached after he had made conservative assumptions about the proportion of the money donated that will actually reach its target.

One genuine difference between Bob and those who can afford to donate to overseas aid organizations but don't is that only Bob can save the child on the tracks, whereas there are hundreds of millions of people who can give $200 to overseas aid organizations. The problem is that most of them aren't doing it. Does this mean that it is all right for you not to do it?

Suppose that there were more owners of priceless vintage cars—Carol, Dave, Emma, Fred, and so on, down to Ziggy—all in exactly the same situation as Bob, with their own siding and their own switch, all sacrificing the child in order to preserve their own cherished car. Would that make it all right for Bob to do the same? To answer this question affirmatively is to endorse follow-the-crowd ethics— the kind of ethics that led many Germans to look away when the Nazi atrocities were being committed. We do not excuse them because others were behaving no better.

We seem to lack a sound basis for drawing a clear moral line between Bob's situation and that of any reader of this article with $200 to spare who does not donate it to an overseas aid agency. These readers seem to be acting at least as badly as Bob was acting when he chose to let the runaway train hurtle toward the unsuspecting child. In the light of this conclusion, I trust that many readers will reach for the phone and donate that $200. Perhaps you should do it before reading further.

◇

Now that you have distinguished yourself morally from people who put their vintage cars ahead of a child's life, how about treating yourself and your partner to dinner at your favorite restaurant? But wait. The money you will spend at the restaurant could also help save the lives of children overseas! True, you weren't planning to blow $200 tonight, but if you were to give up dining out just for one month, you would easily save that amount. And what is one month's dining out, compared to a child's life? There's the rub. Since there are a lot of desperately needy children in the world, there will always be another child whose life you could save for another $200. Are you therefore obliged to keep giving until you have nothing left? At what point can you stop?

Hypothetical examples can easily become farcical. Consider Bob. How far past losing the Bugatti should he go? Imagine that Bob had got his foot stuck in the track of the siding, and if he diverted the train, then before it rammed the car it would also amputate his big toe. Should he still throw the switch? What if it would amputate his foot? His entire leg?

As absurd as the Bugatti scenario gets when pushed to extremes, the point it raises is a serious one: only when the sacrifices become very significant indeed would most people be prepared to say that Bob does nothing wrong when he decides not to throw the switch. Of course, most people could be wrong; we can't decide moral issues by taking opinion polls. But consider for yourself the level of sacrifice that you would demand of Bob, and then think about how much money you would have to give away in order to make a sacrifice that is roughly equal to that. It's almost certainly much, much more than $200. For most middle-class Americans, it could easily be more like $200,000.

Isn't it counterproductive to ask people to do so much? Don't we run the risk that many will shrug their shoulders and say that morality, so conceived, is fine for saints but not for them? I accept that we are unlikely to see, in the near or even medium-term future, a world in which it is normal for wealthy Americans to give the bulk of their wealth to strangers. When it comes to praising or blaming people for what they do, we tend to use a standard that is relative to some conception of normal behavior. Comfortably off Americans who give, say, 10 percent of their income to overseas aid organizations are so far ahead of most of their equally comfortable fellow citizens that I wouldn't go out of my way to chastise them for not doing more. Nevertheless, they should be doing much more, and they are in no position to criticize Bob for failing to make the much greater sacrifice of his Bugatti.

At this point various objections may crop up. Someone may say: "If every citizen living in the affluent nations contributed his or her share I wouldn't have to make such a drastic sacrifice, because long before such levels were reached, the resources would have been there to save the lives of all those children dying from lack of food or medical care. So why should I give more than my fair share?" Another, related, objection is that the Government ought to increase its overseas aid allocations, since that would spread the burden more equitably across all taxpayers.

Yet the question of how much we ought to give is a matter to be decided in the real world—and that, sadly, is a world in which we know that most people do not, and in the immediate future will not, give substantial amounts to overseas aid agencies. We know, too, that at least in the next year, the United States Government is not going to meet even the very modest United Nations–recommended target of .7 percent of gross national product; at the moment it lags far below that, at .09 percent, not even half of Japan's .22 percent or a tenth of Denmark's .97 percent. Thus, we know that the money we can give beyond that theoretical "fair share" is still going to save lives that would otherwise be lost. While the idea that no one need do more than his or her fair share is a powerful one, should it prevail if we know that others are not doing their fair share and that children will die preventable deaths unless we do more than our fair share? That would be taking fairness too far.

Thus, this ground for limiting how much we ought to give also fails. In the world as it is now, I can see no escape from the conclusion that each one of us with wealth surplus to his or her essential needs should be giving most of it to help people suffering from poverty so dire as to be life-threatening. That's right: I'm saying that you shouldn't buy that new car, take that cruise, redecorate the house, or get that pricey new suit. After all, a $1,000 suit could save five children's lives.

So how does my philosophy break down in dollars and cents? An American household with an income of $50,000 spends around $30,000 annually on necessities, according to the Conference Board, a nonprofit economic research organization. Therefore, for a household bringing in $50,000 a year, donations to help the world's poor should be as close as possible to $20,000. The $30,000 required for necessities holds for higher incomes as well. So a household making $100,000 could cut a yearly check for $70,000. Again, the formula is simple: whatever money you're spending on luxuries, not necessities, should be given away.

Now, evolutionary psychologists tell us that human nature just isn't sufficiently altruistic to make it plausible that many people will sacrifice so much for strangers. On the facts of human nature, they might be right, but they would be wrong to draw a moral conclusion from those facts. If it is the case that we ought to do things that, predictably, most of us won't do, then let's face that fact head-on. Then, if we value the life of a child more than going to fancy restaurants, the next time we dine out we will know that we could have done something better with our money. If that makes living a morally decent life extremely arduous, well, then that is the way things are. If we don't do it, then we should at least know that we are failing to live a morally decent life—not because it is good to wallow in guilt but because knowing where we should be going is the first step toward heading in that direction.

When Bob first grasped the dilemma that faced him as he stood by that railway switch, he must have thought how extraordinarily unlucky he was to be placed in a situation in which he must choose between the life of an innocent child and the sacrifice of most of his savings. But he was not unlucky at all. We are all in that situation.

WHAT SHOULD A BILLIONAIRE GIVE—AND WHAT SHOULD YOU?

IN 2006, TWO major news stories focused attention on the philanthropy of billionaires. Bill Gates announced that he would phase out his executive role at Microsoft, and spend more time working with the Bill and Melinda Gates Foundation, already by far the largest charitable foundation in the world, thanks to gifts from Bill and Melinda. Then Warren Buffett announced that he planned to give away most of his $44 billion fortune, including a gift of $31 billion to the Gates Foundation. Ilena Silverman, an

Originally published in The New York Times Sunday Magazine, December 17, 2006.

editor at the *New York Times Sunday Magazine*, asked me to write about some of the ethical questions raised by these massive donations from super-rich individuals. I agreed, but I didn't want to limit the article's scope to what billionaires should do. It appeared just when most U.S. donors are finalizing their charitable giving, before the tax year ends on December 31.

◇

W hat is a human life worth? You may not want to put a price tag on it. But if we really had to, most of us would agree that the value of a human life would be in the millions. Consistent with the foundations of our democracy and our frequently professed belief in the inherent dignity of human beings, we would also agree that all humans are created equal, at least to the extent of denying that differences of sex, ethnicity, nationality, and place of residence change the value of a human life.

With Christmas approaching, and Americans writing checks to their favorite charities, it's a good time to ask how these two beliefs— that a human life, if it can be priced at all, is worth millions, and that the factors I have mentioned do not alter the value of a human life—square with our actions. Perhaps this year such questions lurk beneath the surface of more family discussions than usual, for it has been an extraordinary year for philanthropy, especially philanthropy to fight global poverty.

For Bill Gates, the founder of Microsoft, the ideal of valuing all human life equally began to jar against reality some years ago, when he read an article about diseases in the developing world and came across the statistic that half a million children die every year from rotavirus, the most common cause of severe diarrhea in children. He had never heard of rotavirus. "How could I never have heard of something that kills half a million children every year?" he asked himself. He then learned that in developing countries, millions of children die from diseases that have been eliminated, or virtually eliminated, in the United States. That shocked him because he assumed that, if there are vaccines and treatments that could save lives, governments would be doing everything possible to get them to the people who need them. As Gates told a meeting of the World Health Assembly in Geneva last year, he and his wife, Melinda, "couldn't escape the brutal conclusion that—in our world today—some lives are seen as worth saving and others are not." They said to themselves, "This can't be true." But they knew it was.

Gates's speech to the World Health Assembly concluded on an optimistic note, looking forward to the next decade when "people will finally accept that the death of a child in the developing world is just as tragic as the death of a child in the developed world." That belief in the equal value of all human life is also prominent on the Web site of the Bill and Melinda Gates Foundation, where under Our Values we read: "All lives—no matter where they are being led—have equal value."

We are very far from acting in accordance with that belief. In the same world in which more than a billion people live at a level of affluence never previously known, roughly a billion other people struggle to survive on the purchasing power equivalent of less than one U.S. dollar per day. Most of the world's poorest people are undernourished, lack access to safe drinking water or even the most basic health services, and cannot send their children to school. According to UNICEF, more than 10 million children die every year—about 30,000 per day—from avoidable, poverty-related causes.

Last June the investor Warren Buffett took a significant step toward reducing those deaths when he pledged $31 billion to the Gates Foundation, and another $6 billion to other charitable foundations. Buffett's pledge, set alongside the nearly $30 billion given by Bill and Melinda Gates to their foundation, has made it clear that the first decade of the 21st century is a new "golden age of philanthropy." On an inflation-adjusted basis, Buffett has pledged to give more than double the lifetime total given away by two of the philanthropic giants of the past, Andrew Carnegie and John D. Rockefeller, put together. Bill and Melinda Gates's gifts are not far behind.

The Gates' and Buffett's donations will now be put to work primarily to reduce poverty, disease, and premature death in the developing world. According to the Global Forum for Health Research, less than 10 percent of the world's health research budget is spent on combating conditions that account for 90 percent of the global burden of disease. In the past, diseases that affect only the poor have been of no commercial interest to pharmaceutical manufacturers, because the poor cannot afford to buy their products. The Global Alliance for Vaccines and Immunization (GAVI), heavily supported by the Gates Foundation, seeks to change this by guaranteeing to purchase millions of doses of vaccines, when they are developed, that can prevent diseases like malaria. GAVI has also assisted developing countries to immunize more people with existing vaccines:

99 million additional children have been reached to date. By doing this, GAVI claims to have already averted nearly 1.7 million future deaths.

Philanthropy on this scale raises many ethical questions: Why are the people who are giving doing so? Does it do any good? Should we praise them for giving so much or criticize them for not giving still more? Is it troubling that such momentous decisions are made by a few extremely wealthy individuals? And how do our judgments about them reflect on our own way of living?

Let's start with the question of motives. The rich must—or so some of us with less money like to assume—suffer sleepless nights because of their ruthlessness in squeezing out competitors, firing workers, shutting down plants, or whatever else they have to do to acquire their wealth. When wealthy people give away money, we can always say that they are doing it to ease their consciences or generate favorable publicity. It has been suggested—by, for example, David Kirkpatrick, a senior editor at *Fortune* magazine—that Bill Gates's turn to philanthropy was linked to the antitrust problems Microsoft had in the U.S. and the European Union. Was Gates, consciously or subconsciously, trying to improve his own image and that of his company?

This kind of sniping tells us more about the attackers than the attacked. Giving away large sums, rather than spending the money on corporate advertising or developing new products, is not a sensible strategy for increasing personal wealth. When we read that someone has given away a lot of their money, or time, to help others, it challenges us to think about our own behavior. Should we be following their example, in our own modest way? But if the rich just give their money away to improve their image, or to make up for past misdeeds—misdeeds quite unlike any we have committed, of course—then, conveniently, what they are doing has no relevance to what we ought to do.

A famous story is told about Thomas Hobbes, the 17th-century English philosopher, who argued that we all act in our own interests. On seeing him give alms to a beggar, a cleric asked Hobbes if he would have done this if Christ had not commanded us to do so. Yes, Hobbes replied, he was in pain to see the miserable condition of the old man, and his gift, by providing the man with some relief from that misery, also eased Hobbes's pain. That reply reconciles Hobbes's charity with his egoistic theory of human motivation, but at the cost of emptying egoism of much of its bite. If egoists suffer when they see a stranger in distress, they are capable of being as charitable as any altruist.

Followers of the 18th-century German philosopher Immanuel Kant would disagree. They think an act has moral worth only if it is done out of a sense of duty. Doing something merely because you enjoy doing it, or enjoy seeing its consequences, they say, has no moral worth, because if you happened not to enjoy doing it, then you wouldn't do it, and you are not responsible for your likes and dislikes, whereas you are responsible for your obedience to the demands of duty.

Perhaps some philanthropists are motivated by their sense of duty. Apart from the equal value of all human life, the other "simple value" that lies at the core of the work of the Gates Foundation, according to its Web site, is "To whom much has been given, much is expected." That suggests the view that those who have great wealth have a duty to use it for a larger purpose than their own interests. But while such questions of motive may be relevant to our assessment of Gates's or Buffett's character, they pale into insignificance when we consider the effect of what Gates and Buffett are doing. The parents whose children could die from rotavirus care more about getting the help that will save their children's lives than about the motivations of those who make that possible.

Interestingly, neither Gates nor Buffett seems motivated by the possibility of being rewarded in heaven for his good deeds on earth. Gates told a *Time* interviewer, "There's a lot more I could be doing on a Sunday morning" than going to church. Put them together with

Andrew Carnegie, famous for his freethinking, and three of the four greatest American philanthropists have been atheists or agnostics. (The exception is John D. Rockefeller.) In a country in which 96 percent of the population say they believe in a supreme being, that's a striking fact. It means that in one sense, Gates and Buffett are probably less self-interested in their charity than someone like Mother Teresa, who as a pious Roman Catholic believed in reward and punishment in the afterlife.

More important than questions about motives are questions about whether there is an obligation for the rich to give, and if so, how much they should give. A few years ago, an African-American cabdriver taking me to the Inter-American Development Bank in Washington asked me if I worked at the bank. I told him I did not but was speaking at a conference on development and aid. He then assumed that I was an economist, but when I said no, my training was in philosophy, he asked me if I thought the U.S. should give foreign aid. When I answered affirmatively, he replied that the government shouldn't tax people in order to give their money to others. That, he thought, was robbery. When I asked if he believed that the rich should voluntarily donate some of what they earn to the poor, he said that if someone had worked for his money, he wasn't going to tell him what to do with it.

At that point we reached our destination. Had the journey continued, I might have tried to persuade him that people can earn large amounts only when they live under favorable social circumstances, and that they don't create those circumstances by themselves. I could have quoted Warren Buffett's acknowledgment that society is responsible for much of his wealth. "If you stick me down in the middle of Bangladesh or Peru," he said, "you'll find out how much this talent is going to produce in the wrong kind of soil." The Nobel Prize–winning economist and social scientist Herbert Simon estimated that "social capital" is responsible for at least 90 percent of what people earn in wealthy societies like those of the United States or northwestern Europe. By social capital Simon meant not only natural resources but, more important, the technology and organizational skills in the community, and the presence of good government. These are the foundation on which the rich can begin their work. "On moral grounds," Simon added, "we could argue for a flat income tax of 90 percent." Simon was not, of course, advocating so steep a rate of tax, for he was well aware of disincentive effects. But his estimate does undermine the argument that the rich are entitled to keep their wealth because it is all a result of their hard work. If Simon is right, that is true of at most 10 percent of it.

In any case, even if we were to grant that people deserve every dollar they earn, that doesn't answer the question of what they should do with it. We might say that they have a right to spend it on lavish parties, private jets, and luxury yachts, or, for that matter, to flush it down the toilet. But we could still think that for them to do these things while others die from easily preventable diseases is wrong. In an article I wrote more than three decades ago, at the time of a humanitarian emergency in what is now Bangladesh, I used the example of walking by a shallow pond and seeing a small child who has fallen in and appears to be in danger of drowning. Even though we did nothing to cause the child to fall into the pond, almost everyone agrees that if we can save the child at minimal inconvenience or trouble to ourselves, we ought to do so. Anything else would be callous, indecent, and, in a word, wrong. The fact that in rescuing the child we may, for example, ruin a new pair of shoes is not a good reason for allowing the child to drown. Similarly if for the cost of a pair of shoes we can contribute to a health program in a developing country that stands a good chance of saving the life of a child, we ought to do so.

Perhaps, though, our obligation to help the poor is even stronger than this example implies, for we are less innocent than the passer-by who did nothing to cause the child to fall into the pond. Thomas Pogge, a philosopher at Columbia University, has argued that at least some of our affluence comes at the expense of the poor. He bases this claim not simply on the usual critique of the barriers that Europe and the United States maintain against agricultural imports from developing countries but also on less familiar aspects of our trade with developing countries. For example, he points out that international corporations are willing to make deals to buy natural resources from any government, no matter how it has come to power. This provides a huge financial incentive for groups to try to overthrow the existing government. Successful rebels are rewarded by being able to sell off the nation's oil, minerals, or timber.

In their dealings with corrupt dictators in developing countries, Pogge asserts, international corporations are morally no better than someone who knowingly buys stolen goods—with the difference that the international legal and political order recognizes the corporations, not as criminals in possession of stolen goods but as the legal owners of the goods they have bought. This situation is, of course, beneficial for the industrial nations, because it enables us to obtain the raw materials we need to maintain our prosperity, but it is a disaster for resource-rich developing countries, turning the wealth that should benefit them into a curse that leads to a cycle of coups, civil wars, and corruption and is of little benefit to the people as a whole.

In this light, our obligation to the poor is not just one of providing assistance to strangers but one of compensation for harms that we have caused and are still causing them. It might be argued that we do not owe the poor compensation, because our affluence actually benefits them. Living luxuriously, it is said, provides employment, and so wealth trickles down, helping the poor more effectively than aid does. But the rich in industrialized nations buy virtually nothing that is made by the very poor. During the past 20 years of economic globalization, although expanding trade has helped lift many of the world's poor out of poverty, it has failed to benefit the poorest 10 percent of the world's population. Some of the extremely poor, most of whom live in sub-Saharan Africa, have nothing to sell that rich people want, while others lack the infrastructure to get their goods to market. If they can get their crops to a port, European and U.S. subsidies often mean that they cannot sell them, despite—as for example in the case of West African cotton growers who compete with vastly larger and richer U.S. cotton producers—having a lower production cost than the subsidized producers in the rich nations.

The remedy to these problems, it might reasonably be suggested, should come from the state, not from private philanthropy. When aid comes through the government, everyone who earns above the tax-free threshold contributes something, with more collected from those with greater ability to pay. Much as we may applaud what Gates and Buffett are doing, we can also be troubled by a system that leaves the fate of hundreds of millions of people hanging on the decisions of two or three private citizens. But the amount of foreign development aid given by the U.S. government is, at 22 cents for every $100 the nation earns, about the same, as a percentage of gross national income, as Portugal gives and about half that of the U.K. Worse still, much of it is directed where it best suits U.S. strategic interests—Iraq is now by far the largest recipient of U.S. development aid, and Egypt, Jordan, Pakistan, and Afghanistan all rank in the Top 10. Less than a quarter of official U.S. development aid—barely a nickel in every $100 of our G.N.I.—goes to the world's poorest nations.

Adding private philanthropy to U.S. government aid improves this picture, because Americans privately give more per capita to international philanthropic causes than the citizens of almost any other nation. Even when private donations are included, however, countries like Norway, Denmark, Sweden, and the Netherlands give three or four times as much foreign aid, in proportion to the size of their economies, as the U.S. gives—with a much larger percentage going to the poorest nations. At least as things now stand, the case for philanthropic efforts to relieve global poverty is not susceptible to the argument that the government has taken care of the problem. And even if official U.S. aid were better-directed and comparable, relative to our gross domestic product, with that of the most generous nations, there would still be a role for private philanthropy. Unconstrained by diplomatic considerations or the desire to swing votes at the United Nations, private donors can more easily avoid dealing with corrupt or wasteful governments. They can go directly into the field, working with local villages and grass-roots organizations.

Nor are philanthropists beholden to lobbyists. As the *New York Times* reported recently, billions of dollars of U.S. aid is tied to domestic goods. Wheat for Africa must be grown in America, although aid experts say this often depresses local African markets, reducing the incentive for farmers there to produce more. In a decision that surely costs lives, hundreds of millions of condoms intended to stop the spread of AIDS in Africa and around the world must be manufactured in the U.S., although they cost twice as much as similar products made in Asia.

In other ways, too, private philanthropists are free to venture where governments fear to tread. Through a foundation named for his wife, Susan Thompson Buffett, Warren Buffett has supported reproductive rights, including family planning and pro-choice organizations. In another unusual initiative, he has pledged $50 million for the International Atomic Energy Agency's plan to establish a "fuel bank" to supply nuclear-reactor fuel to countries that meet their nuclear-nonproliferation commitments. The idea, which has been talked about for many years, is widely agreed to be a useful step toward discouraging countries from building their own facilities for producing nuclear fuel, which could then be diverted to weapons production. It is, Buffett said, "an investment in a safer world." Though it is something that governments could and should be doing, no government had taken the first step.

Aid has always had its critics. Carefully planned and intelligently directed private philanthropy may be the best answer to the claim that aid doesn't work. Of course, as in any large-scale human enterprise, some aid can be ineffective. But provided that aid isn't actually counterproductive, even relatively inefficient assistance is likely to do more to advance human well-being than luxury spending by the wealthy.

◊

The rich, then, should give. But how much should they give? Gates may have given away nearly $30 billion, but that still leaves him sitting at the top of the *Forbes* list of the richest Americans, with $53 billion. His 66,000-square-foot high-tech lakeside estate near Seattle is reportedly worth more than $100 million. Property taxes are about $1 million. Among his possessions is the Leicester Codex, the only handwritten book by Leonardo da Vinci still in private hands, for which he paid $30.8 million in 1994. Has Bill Gates done enough?

More pointedly, you might ask: if he really believes that all lives have equal value, what is he doing living in such an expensive house and owning a Leonardo Codex? Are there no more lives that could be saved by living more modestly and adding the money thus saved to the amount he has already given?

Yet we should recognize that, if judged by the proportion of his wealth that he has given away, Gates compares very well with most of the other people on the *Forbes* 400 list, including his former colleague and Microsoft co-founder, Paul Allen. Allen, who left the company in 1983, has given, over his lifetime, more than $800 million to philanthropic causes. That is far more than nearly any of us will ever be able to give. But *Forbes* lists Allen as the fifth-richest American, with a net worth of $16 billion. He owns the Seattle Seahawks, the Portland Trailblazers, and a 413-foot oceangoing yacht that carries two helicopters and a 60-foot submarine. He has given only about 5 percent of his total wealth.

Is there a line of moral adequacy that falls between the 5 percent that Allen has given away and the roughly 35 percent that Gates has donated? Few people have set a personal example that would allow them to tell Gates that he has not given enough, but one who could is Zell Kravinsky. A few years ago, when he was in his mid-40s, Kravinsky gave almost all of his $45 million real estate fortune to health-related charities, retaining only his modest family home in Jenkintown, near Philadelphia, and enough to meet his family's ordinary expenses. After learning that thousands of people with failing kidneys die each year while waiting for a transplant, he contacted a Philadelphia hospital and donated one of his kidneys to a complete stranger.

After reading about Kravinsky in the *New Yorker*, I invited him to speak to my classes at Princeton. He comes across as anguished by the failure of others to see the simple logic that lies behind his altruism. Kravinsky has a mathematical mind—a talent that obviously helped him in deciding what investments would prove profitable—and he says that the chances of dying as a result of donating a kidney are about 1 in 4,000. For him this implies that to withhold a kidney from someone who would otherwise die means valuing one's own life at 4,000 times that of a stranger, a ratio Kravinsky considers "obscene."

What marks Kravinsky from the rest of us is that he takes the equal value of all human life as a guide to life, not just as a nice piece of rhetoric. He acknowledges that some people think he is crazy, and even his wife says she believes that he goes too far. One of her arguments against the kidney donation was that one of their children may one day need a kidney, and Zell could be the only compatible donor. Kravinsky's love for his children is, as far as I can tell, as strong as that of any normal parent. Such attachments are part of our nature, no doubt the product of our evolution as mammals who give birth to children, who for an unusually long time require our assistance in order to survive. But that does not, in Kravinsky's view, justify our placing a value on the lives of our children that is thousands of times greater than the value we place on the lives of the children of strangers. Asked if he would allow his child to die if it would enable a thousand children to live, Kravinsky said yes. Indeed, he has said he would permit his child to die even if this enabled only two other children to live. Nevertheless, to appease his wife, he recently went back into real estate, made some money, and bought the family a larger home. But he still remains committed to giving away as much as possible, subject only to keeping his domestic life reasonably tranquil.

Buffett says he believes in giving his children "enough so they feel they could do anything, but not so much that they could do nothing." That means, in his judgment, "a few hundred thousand" each. In absolute terms, that is far more than most Americans are able to leave their children and, by Kravinsky's standard, certainly too much. (Kravinsky says that the hard part is not giving away the first $45 million but the last $10,000, when you have to live so cheaply that you can't function in the business world.) But even if Buffett left each of his three children a million dollars each, he would still have given away more than 99.99 percent of his wealth. When someone does that much—especially in a society in which the norm is to leave most of your wealth to your children—it is better to praise them than to cavil about the extra few hundred thousand dollars they might have given.

Philosophers like Liam Murphy of New York University and my colleague Kwame Anthony Appiah at Princeton contend that our obligations are limited to carrying our fair share of the burden of relieving global poverty. They would have us calculate how much would be required to ensure that the world's poorest people have a chance at a decent life, and then divide this sum among the affluent. That would give us each an amount to donate, and having given that, we would have fulfilled our obligations to the poor.

What might that fair amount be? One way of calculating it would be to take as our target, at least for the next nine years, the Millennium Development Goals, set by the United Nations Millennium Summit in 2000. On that occasion, the largest gathering of world leaders in history jointly pledged to meet, by 2015, a list of goals that include:

Reducing by half the proportion of the world's people in extreme poverty (defined as living on less than the purchasing-power equivalent of one U.S. dollar per day).

Reducing by half the proportion of people who suffer from hunger.

Ensuring that children everywhere are able to take a full course of primary schooling.

Ending sex disparity in education.

Reducing by two-thirds the mortality rate among children under 5.

Reducing by three-quarters the rate of maternal mortality.

Halting and beginning to reverse the spread of H.I.V./AIDS and halting and beginning to reduce the incidence of malaria and other major diseases.

Reducing by half the proportion of people without sustainable access to safe drinking water.

Last year a United Nations task force, led by the Columbia University economist Jeffrey Sachs, estimated the annual cost of meeting these goals to be $121 billion in 2006, rising to $189 billion by 2015. When we take account of existing official development aid promises, the additional amount needed each year to meet the goals is only $48 billion for 2006 and $74 billion for 2015.

Now let's look at the incomes of America's rich and superrich, and ask how much they could reasonably give. The task is made easier by statistics recently provided by Thomas Piketty and Emmanuel Saez, economists at the École Normale Supérieure, Paris-Jourdan, and the University of California, Berkeley, respectively, based on U.S. tax data for 2004. Their figures are for pretax income, excluding income from capital gains, which for the very rich are nearly always substantial. For simplicity I have rounded the figures, generally downward. Note too that the numbers refer to "tax units," that is, in many cases, families rather than individuals.

Piketty and Saez's top bracket comprises .01 percent of U.S. taxpayers. There are 14,400 of them, earning an average of $12,775,000, with total earnings of $184 billion. The minimum annual income in this group is more than $5 million, so it seems reasonable to suppose that they could, without much hardship, give away a third of their annual income, an average of $4.3 million each, for a total of around $61 billion. That would still leave each of them with an annual income of at least $3.3 million.

Next comes the rest of the top .1 percent (excluding the category just described, as I shall do henceforth). There are 129,600 in this group, with an average income of just over $2 million and a minimum income of $1.1 million. If they were each to give a quarter of their income, that would yield about $65 billion, and leave each of them with at least $846,000 annually.

The top .5 percent consists of 575,900 taxpayers, with an average income of $623,000 and a minimum of $407,000. If they were to give one-fifth of their income, they would still have at least $325,000 each, and they would be giving a total of $72 billion.

Coming down to the level of those in the top 1 percent, we find 719,900 taxpayers with an average income of $327,000 and a minimum of $276,000. They could comfortably afford to give 15 percent of their income. That would yield $35 billion and leave them with at least $234,000.

Finally, the remainder of the nation's top 10 percent earn at least $92,000 annually, with an average of $132,000. There are nearly 13 million in this group. If they gave the traditional tithe—10 percent of their income, or an average of $13,200 each—this would yield about $171 billion and leave them a minimum of $83,000.

You could spend a long time debating whether the fractions of income I have suggested for donation constitute the fairest possible scheme. Perhaps the sliding scale should be steeper, so that the superrich give more and the merely comfortable give less. And it could be extended beyond the Top 10 percent of American families, so that everyone able to afford more than the basic necessities of life gives something, even if it is as little as 1 percent. Be that as it may, the remarkable thing about these calculations is that a scale of donations that is unlikely to impose significant hardship on anyone yields a total of $404 billion—from just 10 percent of American families.

Obviously, the rich in other nations should share the burden of relieving global poverty. The U.S. is responsible for 36 percent of the gross domestic product of all Organization for Economic Cooperation and Development nations. Arguably, because the U.S. is richer than all other major nations, and its wealth is more unevenly distributed than wealth in almost any other industrialized country, the rich in the U.S. should contribute more than 36 percent of total global donations. So somewhat more than 36 percent of all aid to relieve global poverty should come from the U.S. For simplicity, let's take half as a fair share for the U.S. On that basis, extending the scheme I have suggested worldwide would provide $808 billion annually for development aid. That's more than six times what the task force chaired by Sachs estimated would be required for 2006 in order to be on track to meet the Millennium Development Goals, and more than 16 times the shortfall between that sum and existing official development aid commitments.

If we are obliged to do no more than our fair share of eliminating global poverty, the burden will not be great. But is that really all we ought to do? Since we all agree that fairness is a good thing, and none of us like doing more because others don't pull their weight, the fair-share view is attractive. In the end, however, I think we should reject it. Let's return to the drowning child in the shallow pond. Imagine it is not 1 small child who has fallen in, but 50 children. We are among 50 adults, unrelated to the children, picnicking on the lawn around the pond. We can easily wade into the pond and rescue the children, and the fact that we would find it cold and unpleasant sloshing around in the knee-deep muddy water is no justification for failing to do so. The "fair share" theorists would say that if we each rescue one child, all the children will be saved, and so none of us have an obligation to save more than one. But what if half the picnickers prefer staying clean and dry to rescuing any children at all? Is it acceptable if the rest of us stop after we have rescued just one child, knowing that we have done our fair share, but that half the children will drown? We might justifiably be furious with those who are not doing their fair share, but our anger with them is not a reason for letting the children die. In terms of praise and blame, we are clearly right to condemn, in the strongest terms, those who do nothing. In contrast, we may withhold such condemnation from those who stop when they have done their fair share. Even so, they have let children drown when they could easily have saved them, and that is wrong.

Similarly, in the real world, it should be seen as a serious moral failure when those with ample income do not do their fair share toward relieving global poverty. It isn't so easy, however, to decide on the proper approach to take to those who limit their contribution to their fair share when they could easily do more and when, because others are not playing their part, a further donation would assist many in desperate need. In the privacy of our own judgment, we should believe that it is wrong not to do more. But whether we should actually criticize people who are doing their fair share, but no more than that, depends on the psychological impact that such criticism will have on them, and on others. This in turn may depend on social practices. If the majority are doing little or nothing, setting a standard higher than the fair-share level may seem so demanding that it discourages people who are willing to make an equitable contribution from doing even that. So it may be best to refrain from criticizing those who achieve the fair-share level. In moving our society's standards forward, we may have to progress one step at a time.

For more than 30 years, I've been reading, writing, and teaching about the ethical issue posed by the juxtaposition, on our planet, of great abundance and life-threatening poverty. Yet it was not until, in preparing this essay, I calculated how much America's Top 10 percent of income earners actually make that I fully understood how easy it would be for the world's rich to eliminate, or virtually eliminate, global poverty. (It has actually become much easier over the last 30 years, as the rich have grown significantly richer.) I found the result astonishing. I double-checked the figures and asked a research assistant to check them as well. But they were right. Measured against our capacity, the Millennium Development

Goals are indecently, shockingly modest. If we fail to achieve them—as on present indications we well might—we have no excuses. The target we should be setting for ourselves is not halving the proportion of people living in extreme poverty, and without enough to eat, but ensuring that no one, or virtually no one, needs to live in such degrading conditions. That is a worthy goal, and it is well within our reach.